The MISSISSIPPI

Michael Pollard

*B*ENCHMARK *B*OOKS

MARSHALL CAVENDISH
NEW YORK

Benchmark Books
Marshall Cavendish Corporation
99 White Plains Road
Tarrytown, New York 10591-9001

American edition © Marshall Cavendish Corporation 1998

First published in 1997 by Evans Brothers Limited
© Evans Brothers Limited 1997

Library of Congress Cataloging-in-Publication Data
Pollard, Michael, date.
    The Mississippi / Michael Pollard.
        p. cm. — (Great rivers)
    Includes bibliographical references and index.
    Summary: Traces the course of the river Mark Twain
immortalized; describes its physical features, history, and
importance.
        ISBN 0-7614-0502-X (lib. bdg.)
        1. Mississippi River—Juvenile literature.
    [1. Mississippi River] I. Title. II. Series: Pollard,
Michael, date. Great rivers.
    F351.P65 1998
    977—dc21   97-17018
                                                     CIP
                                                      AC

Printed in Hong Kong

ACKNOWLEDGEMENTS

For permission to reproduce copyright material, the author
and publishers gratefully acknowledge the following:

Cover: (top) Spectrum Colour Library (left) Hans
Reinhard/Tony Stone Images (right) Steven Allan/Spectrum
Colour Library
Title page: Images Colour Library
page 8 (left) Fred Mayer (right) NASA/Science Photo
Library **page 10** Dorothy Burrows/Eye Ubiquitous **page 11**
(top) Andrew Sacks/Tony Stone (bottom) Chinch
Gryniewicz/Ecoscene **page 12** Peter Newark's Western
Americana **page 13** (left) Cahokia Mounds State Historic
Site (right) Peter Newark's Western America **page 14** Peter
Newark's Western Americana **page 15** (top) Erwin and
Peggy Bauer/Bruce Coleman Limited (bottom) The Image
Bank **page 16** Peter Newark's Western Americana **page 17**
Peter Newark's Western Americana **page 18** Peter Newark's
Western Americana **page 19** (left) Library of
Congress/Corbis (right) Mark Twain Home and Museum,
Hannibal, Missouri **page 20** Andrea Pistolesi/The Image
Bank **page 21** Hans Reinhard/Tony Stone Images **page 22**
Laurence Fordyce/Eye Ubiquitous **page 23** Images Colour
Library **page 24** Kenneth Jarecke/Colorific **page 25** Geoff
Renner/Robert Harding Picture Library **page 26**
Winkley/Ecoscene **page 27** (top) Annie Griffiths Belt/Corbis
(bottom) Images Colour Library **page 28** Images Colour
Library **page 29** Doug McKay/Tony Stone Images **page 30**
(left) Andy Sacks/Tony Stone Images (right) M
Mackenzie/Trip **page 31** (top) Spectrum Colour Library (bot-
tom)Philip Gould/Corbis **page 32** (top) Laurence
Fordyce/Eye Ubiquitous (bottom) James Davis Travel
Photography **page 33** (top) James Davis Travel Photography
(bottom) Fred Mayer/Magnum **page 34** (top) Philip
Gould/Corbis (bottom)Randy Wells/Tony Stone Images **page
35** (top) Steven Allan/Spectrum Colour Library (bottom)
Spectrum Colour Library **page 36** (top) Bob Krist/Tony
Stone Images (bottom) Spectrum Colour Library **page 37**
Images Colour Library **page 38** Images Colour Library **page
39** (top) Dr P. Evans/Bruce Coleman Limited (bottom) Lynn
M. Stone/The Image Bank **page 40** (left) C. Lockwood/Bruce
Coleman Limited (right) Philip Gould/Corbis **page 41**Philip
Gould/Corbis **page 42** John Lewis Stage/The Image Bank
page 43 G. A. Rossi/The Image Bank

CONTENTS

THE BIG RIVER

THE MISSISSIPPI COLLECTS WATER FROM ABOUT ONE-THIRD OF THE AREA OF THE UNITED STATES, FROM THE ROCKIES IN THE WEST TO THE APPALACHIANS IN THE EAST.

▲*In this infra-red photograph the old loops of the river are shown in brown. They have now dried up.*

▲*The Mississippi flows slowly in wide loops through northern Minnesota. Eventually the river will cut through the head of each loop, creating an island and then an ox-bow lake.*

THE MISSISSIPPI AND MISSOURI

Mississippi
   Length: 2350 mi (3780 km)
   Source: Lake Itasca, Minnesota
   Mouth: Mississippi Delta, Gulf of Mexico

Missouri
   Length: 2566 mi (4130 km)
   Source: Three Forks, Montana
   Confluence: near St Louis, Missouri

THE NAME "MISSISSIPPI" comes from the Chippewa Indian word *Meschasipi*, which means "the Big River." Spanish explorers translated this into their own language and called it Rio Grande, but they also gave this name to another river to the west, on the Mexican border. English-speaking settlers turned the Indian name into "Mississippi." Americans who live next to the river or work on it call it simply "the river."

FORTY TRIBUTARIES

The Mississippi flows south across the United States from close to the Canadian border to the Gulf of Mexico, 2350 miles (3780 kilometers) away. At St. Louis it is joined from the west by the Missouri river. Although the Missouri is a tributary, it is about 217 miles (350 kilometers) longer than the Mississippi. From its source in the Rocky Mountains to St. Louis

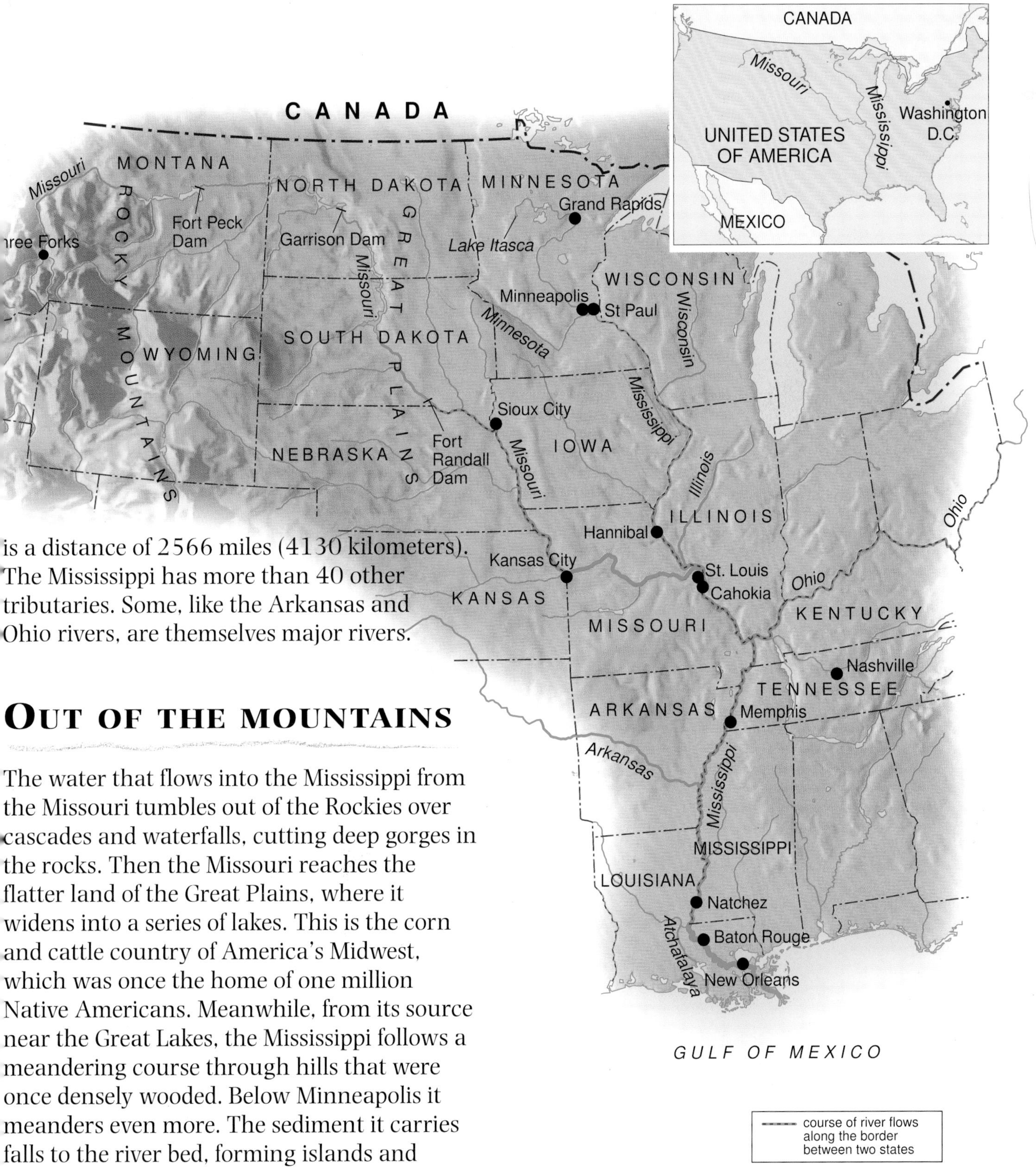
CANADA
UNITED STATES OF AMERICA
MEXICO
Washington D.C.
Missouri
Mississippi
CANADA
MONTANA
NORTH DAKOTA
MINNESOTA
SOUTH DAKOTA
WYOMING
NEBRASKA
IOWA
WISCONSIN
ILLINOIS
KANSAS
MISSOURI
KENTUCKY
TENNESSEE
ARKANSAS
MISSISSIPPI
LOUISIANA
ROCKY MOUNTAINS
GREAT PLAINS
Three Forks
Fort Peck Dam
Garrison Dam
Fort Randall Dam
Grand Rapids
Lake Itasca
Minneapolis
St Paul
Sioux City
Hannibal
Kansas City
St. Louis
Cahokia
Nashville
Memphis
Natchez
Baton Rouge
New Orleans
Missouri
Minnesota
Wisconsin
Mississippi
Illinois
Ohio
Arkansas
Atchafalaya
GULF OF MEXICO
course of river flows along the border between two states

is a distance of 2566 miles (4130 kilometers). The Mississippi has more than 40 other tributaries. Some, like the Arkansas and Ohio rivers, are themselves major rivers.

Out of the Mountains

The water that flows into the Mississippi from the Missouri tumbles out of the Rockies over cascades and waterfalls, cutting deep gorges in the rocks. Then the Missouri reaches the flatter land of the Great Plains, where it widens into a series of lakes. This is the corn and cattle country of America's Midwest, which was once the home of one million Native Americans. Meanwhile, from its source near the Great Lakes, the Mississippi follows a meandering course through hills that were once densely wooded. Below Minneapolis it meanders even more. The sediment it carries falls to the river bed, forming islands and semicircular ox-bow lakes. Finally, having collected all the water from its tributaries, the Mississippi reaches the Gulf of Mexico.

Unknown Country

Until less than 200 years ago, the Mississippi was a great barrier that divided the states of eastern America from the wide open spaces to the west. When people began to cross the river and settle in the land beyond it, the history of North America changed. Even today, the Mississippi and its tributaries flow for most of their length past isolated farms and small towns where life is far different from the America of the big cities.

THE MAKING OF THE RIVERS

THE MISSISSIPPI AND MISSOURI AS THEY ARE TODAY WERE CREATED BY CHANGES IN THE EARTH'S SURFACE WHICH TOOK PLACE OVER MILLIONS OF YEARS.

ABOUT 100 MILLION YEARS AGO, as the Earth's crust cooled, it split into several pieces, or "plates." Two of these were the Pacific Plate, stretching across the present Pacific Ocean to Asia, and the North American Plate, which covered North America and the western Atlantic. These two plates met off the coast of what is now California. The collision of these two huge masses pushed up a range of fold mountains that runs down the west coast of North America. These mountains are known as the Rockies.

The Rockies prevented North America's major rivers from flowing into the Pacific. The result was that the upper Mississippi flowed northwards into a huge lake where the five Great Lakes on the borders of Canada and the United States are today. The Missouri flowed even further north, into Hudson Bay in northern Canada. The Gulf of Mexico extended up to the Ohio river.

▲ *The Rocky Mountains in Montana, where the Mississippi's main tributary, the Missouri, has its source.*

Glaciers advancing southwards carried billions of tons of rock and soil, killing all the plant and animal life in their path. In North America, the glaciers reached as far as the Ohio river valley, where they met the waters of the Gulf of Mexico.

The ice began to retreat about 10,000 years ago. As the ice melted, it left behind the rock and soil it had carried. This glacial material dammed up the old river valleys and partly filled the great lakes. The rivers were forced to find new ways to the sea and new lakes were created in Minnesota and northwestern Canada.

The Mississippi found a route to the south, where it was joined by the Missouri and its other tributaries. The melting ice poured down the rivers, carrying with it loose material that the glaciers had left behind. Some of this material sank to the river bed or was left on the river banks, creating rich, fertile land. This is now the farmland of the riverside states of Mississippi, Tennessee, Louisiana, Arkansas and Missouri. Some sediment was carried further downriver towards the Gulf of Mexico and deposited there. Mud banks built up in the slow-flowing

THE GREAT ICE-CAP

About one million years ago, the sheet of ice covering the North Pole began to spread.

▶ *Harvesting the wheat crop in Minnesota. The "corn belt" of the United States crosses the Missouri and upper Mississippi.*

water and formed swamps covered with thick, tangled plants. When the Mississippi reached the sea the climate was warm, wet and sub-tropical. As the river's delta grew, it became the home of swamp-dwelling creatures such as alligators and poisonous snakes.

MAIN TRIBUTARIES OF THE MISSISSIPPI

Wisconsin: 600 mi (965 km) joins near Prairie du Chien, Wisconsin
Minnesota: 450 mi (725 km) joins near Minneapolis, Minnesota
Missouri: 2566 mi(4130 km) joins near St. Louis, Missouri
Ohio: 982 mi (1580 km) joins at Cairo, Illinois
Illinois: 497 mi (800 km) joins near Alton, Illinois
Arkansas: 2001 mi (3220 km) joins near Greenville, Mississippi

---

▼ *One of the many bayous, or channels, along which water from the Mississippi flows across the delta to the Gulf of Mexico. The bayous are lined with rich subtropical vegetation.*

THE FIRST AMERICANS

THE BERING STRAIT, A NARROW SEA CHANNEL BETWEEN NORTHEASTERN ASIA AND ALASKA, IS ONLY 56 MILES (90 KILOMETERS) WIDE. THOUSANDS OF YEARS AGO, PEOPLE CROSSED THE STRAIT TO BECOME THE FIRST AMERICANS.

▲ A Sioux family in the 1880s on a US government reservation in South Dakota. The canvas tent behind them has been provided by the government. In the background is a traditional Sioux tepee.

THE NEWCOMERS WERE HUNTERS who moved around in search of food for themselves and their animals. In about 1000 BC some of their descendants began to settle and farm the land of the Mississippi and Ohio river valleys.

PEOPLE OF THE MOUNDS

Unlike the Ancient Egyptians, these early farmers left no written history behind them.

All that is known is that from about AD 800 they built earth mounds. Some seem to have been forts and others were temples or burial-places. There are thousands of mounds scattered across the United States, from the Great Lakes to the Gulf of Mexico, but the largest numbers are in the valleys of the Mississippi and its tributaries. Archaeologists believe that the capital of this civilization was at Cahokia, near St. Louis, where as many as 20,000 people lived.

No one knows why, by about AD 1500, the

▼ *Monks Mound, the largest of the Cahokia Mounds near Collinsville, Illinois, 8 miles (13 kilometers) east of St. Louis and the Mississippi. A building 105 feet (32 meters) long and 49 feet (15 meters) wide once stood on the Mound and it was from there that the chief of Cahokia ruled over his city of 20,000 people.*

NATIVE AMERICANS TODAY

In 1990 the largest groups of Native Americans were Cherokees (350,000), Navajos (230,000), Chippewas, or Ojibwe, (110,000) and Sioux, also called Dakota Indians (110,000). The Sioux were the largest group on the Mississippi and Missouri. About 35,000 lived in reservations in South Dakota, 2000 in Montana, and smaller numbers in Nebraska, Minnesota and North Dakota.

▼ *The Battle of Wounded Knee in South Dakota, on December 29, 1890. A force of US cavalry attacked a peaceful gathering of Sioux and killed over 200, including women and children.*

civilization that built the mounds had died out. It could be that there were disastrous floods that destroyed the settlements, or that the people were struck down by disease. The one million Native Americans who were living on the plains when European explorers arrived in the sixteenth century were the descendants of the first Americans, but their way of life was very different. Some, like the Chickasaw Indians who lived along the upper Mississippi, were farmers who lived in permanent villages. Others, such as the Sioux Indians who lived in Minnesota before being driven westward by white settlers, were nomads who lived in tepees. They were hunters and raiders.

THE FATE OF THE NATIVE AMERICANS

Native Americans soon found out that the Europeans had not come to share North America but to take it over. The early Spanish explorers looted their food stocks and drove the Native Americans back by setting fire to

their villages. It was the beginning of nearly 400 years in which the indigenous people were hunted down and steadily driven off their land.

There are about two million Native Americans in the United States today. About 450,000 of them live in reservations - areas specially marked out for them by the government - but many have moved to the cities in search of work. According to the United States' government, about 30 per cent of Native Americans are classed as poor and have little chance of sharing in the prosperous American society they see around them.

THE JOURNEY OUT WEST

UNTIL 1803, ALL THE STATES OF THE USA WERE EAST OF THE
MISSISSIPPI. ACROSS THE RIVER WAS UNKNOWN TERRITORY,
WHICH SETTLERS CALLED "THE WILDERNESS."

"THE WILDERNESS" WAS FRENCH TERRITORY until 1803, when the French Emperor Napoleon sold it to the United States. This more than doubled the area of the United States and extended it to the Rockies. So the American government had to make maps of the land it had bought and it wanted to see if there was an overland route to the Pacific Ocean.

THE ADVENTURES OF LEWIS AND CLARK

On May 14, 1804 a US Army expedition, led by Captains Meriwether Lewis and William Clark, set out from St. Louis up the Missouri. They were still on the upper Missouri when winter set in. They camped for the winter and then set off again. At last, on November 7,

1805, they had their first sight of the Pacific. They camped again for the winter, and it was not until September 1806 that they got back to St. Louis.

Lewis and Clark brought back news of a wonderful country of wide plains full of herds of buffalo and deer, wild fruit of all kinds, and huge catches of freshwater fish. Soon the first pioneer wagons were rolling westwards, crossing the Mississippi on rafts.

Meanwhile, another US Army expedition led by Lieutenant Zebulon Pike was exploring the upper Mississippi. On his return to base at St. Louis in 1806, he reported that in the north, close to the Canadian border, there was another wonderful country, a land rich in pine forests and wildlife. Loggers, fur-traders and trappers began to move in this direction.

TRAVELING WEST

Improvements in technology encouraged the move westwards. By the 1820s, steamships were carrying settlers up the Mississippi as far as St. Louis. In 1855, the first road bridge across the Mississippi, at Minneapolis, was opened. In 1869 the first east-west railroad across the United States, crossing the Mississippi at St. Louis and the Missouri at Kansas City, was completed. In 1862 the US government passed the Homestead Act, giving

◀ *In this painting Lewis and Clark's Indian guide, Sacajawea, shows them the way through the Rocky Mountains. Meriwether Lewis is standing beside her, with William Clark in the background.*

SLAUGHTER OF THE BISON

The bison, or North American buffalo, was the animal that suffered most from the opening up of the West. Until the settlers arrived, about 80 million bison roamed the prairies in herds that sometimes numbered 3000. They provided Native Americans with meat, skins for clothing and shelter, and bones to make tools. The settlers cleared the land for cattle and corn. By 1890, there were only 1000 bison left. They are now protected in national and state parks, and small herds are thriving again.

families settling beyond the Mississippi 65-hectare plots of land - about ¼ square mile (two-thirds of a square kilometer) - to farm. By 1900, over half a million families had taken up the offer.

GAINERS AND LOSERS

For many families, the move west was the start of a new and prosperous life. Others had less success. They borrowed money for seed and tools from the banks, and if their crops failed they found themselves deeply in debt. Railroad companies charged high rates for carrying grain and animals to the markets in the east. Some families could not stand the hardships and loneliness of life in the west and they returned home. Their land was taken over by the more successful farmers, who could afford equipment for cutting and binding corn.

◀ *Settlers on their way westward make camp on the prairie. On the way they have bought herds of sheep and longhorn cattle to stock their new homestead. This contemporary picture shows the homesteaders full of hope and optimism. For many, disappointment lay ahead.*

RIVERS OF TRADE

As the land beyond the Mississippi and Missouri was opened up by settlers, the rivers were no longer barriers. They became vital channels of transport.

THE FIRST JOURNEYS down the Mississippi were made by barges or flatboats, but few sailors were brave enough to attempt the journey upstream. The currents were too strong. But in 1807, two years after the two rivers were explored by US Army expeditions, the first successful American steamboat was built. Four years later, the first steamboat appeared on the Mississippi, and by 1822 there were 35 at work on the river. From 1830 there were steamboats on the Missouri too.

THE GROWTH OF ST. LOUIS

For 30 years, until the railroads had reached the Mississippi and Missouri and bridged them, steamboats were the best means of transport available for passengers and cargoes. Along the river banks there were wharves where cargoes were collected for shipment, and others where fuel for the steamboats was stored. St. Louis was the first city to be created by the river trade. Its population of about 2500 more than doubled between 1815 and 1821, and by 1840 it had almost trebled. By 1860 there were over 5000 steamboats a year using the city's docks.

From 1834 boats could steam up the Mississippi as far as Minneapolis, where their way was blocked by waterfalls. New Orleans, near the mouth of the Mississippi, became the

STERNWHEELERS ON THE MISSISSIPPI

A special design of paddle-steamer, the sternwheeler, was designed in 1814 for use in the shallow waters of the Mississippi. Most paddle-steamers had paddle-wheels in the middle of the boat on each side of a deep hull, with about half of each wheel cutting into the water. Sternwheelers had shallow hulls and just one wide paddle-wheel, at the stern. The depth of the wheel in the water was less than with side wheels. The single paddle at the stern also made the sternwheeler more maneuverable in the confined waters of the river.

◄ *A sternwheeler paddle-steamer on the Mississippi in the 1880s. Sternwheelers were the river's "workhorses," carrying passengers and goods.*

▲ *Before steamboats arrived on the Mississippi, flatboats carried cargoes on the river. Propelled by oars, they were flat-bottomed so that they were less likely to be grounded in shallow water.*

port where the cotton harvest was loaded for shipment to Europe. At Sioux City on the Missouri, the first steamboat arrived from St. Louis in 1854 and the city started to grow at a fast rate.

Although the railways took a great deal of trade from the steamboats, steam traffic on the rivers lingered on until, in the 1930s, diesel tugs began to replace steamboats and a new age of Mississippi transport was born (see pages 22-23).

THE LOGGING TRADE

The growth of the United States created a huge demand for timber. Houses in the West were built of wood, and the railroads also needed timber for sleepers, or ties, between the rails. From about 1830 until 1900, the pine forests of the upper Mississippi were almost destroyed by the greed for wood. Loggers worked through the summer cutting down the trees and they spent the winter hauling the logs on sleds to the river. When the ice melted in spring, the logs were floated downriver in rafts. After about 1870, steam tugs took over and pushed the rafts downstream to the sawmills in Minneapolis. It took 40 days to complete the journey from Grand Rapids – a distance of 323 miles (520 kilometers).

◀ *Tough, powerful diesel-engined tugboats like Mr. Bucky assemble and push-tow today's barge traffic.*

TALES OF THE RIVER

FOR THE EARLY EXPLORERS AND SETTLERS, LIFE ALONG THE
MISSISSIPPI WAS FRAUGHT WITH DANGER AND ADVENTURE.

THE SEARCH FOR EL DORADO

THE FIRST EUROPEAN EXPLORERS of North America were Spanish. They had heard of a legend that somewhere in either North or South America there was a city of untold wealth, El Dorado, where vast hoards of gold, silver and precious stones were to be found. Some Spanish explorers searched for it in South America. One, called Hernando de Soto, decided to look for El Dorado further north.

In 1539 he landed with 730 soldiers in what is now Florida. Over the next two years the Spanish force marched north and then north-west, killing and robbing the Native Americans they met. They were convinced that the native peoples knew the secret of El Dorado, and tortured them for information. Hoping to get rid of the invaders, the Native Americans made up stories about the magic city, sending the Spaniards deeper and deeper into unknown land. At last, without having found El Dorado, de Soto reached the Mississippi near the present-day city of Memphis. His men were exhausted. Half of them had died from disease or in battle. The remainder, still driven on by the thought of riches, crossed the river and marched into Arkansas. They found nothing but an empty land.

In the spring of 1542, de Soto's men arrived back at the Mississippi. There, de Soto caught a fever and died. His disheartened troops decided to end the mission. That summer they built barges and floated them down the river to the sea. Of the 730 men who had set out, fewer than 300 returned.

DANIEL BOONE

Much of the work of opening up trails into the West was done by lone pioneers who became known as "frontiersmen." One of the most famous was Daniel Boone, who was born in Pennsylvania in

▼ *The burial of Hernando de Soto, the Spanish explorer of the lower Mississippi, in 1542 after he had died of fever.*

▶ *Mark Twain's boyhood home in Hannibal, on the Mississippi. He lived there from the age of four until he was eighteen. The fence on the right inspired the opening scene of his story* The Adventures of Tom Sawyer, *when Tom is told by his aunt to paint it.*

◀ *A famous incident from the life of Daniel Boone painted in 1851. He rescues his daughter who has been captured.*

MARK TWAIN

1734. He founded the famous "Wilderness Trail" from Virginia, which was followed by settlers along the Ohio River in Kentucky. Then, in 1799 - six years before Lewis and Clark's expedition - he set out to explore further west. With his sons Nathan and Daniel, he traveled by dug-out canoe down the Ohio river and up the Mississippi to St. Louis, which was then a small trading post for fur-trappers. He went on up the Missouri and founded the town of Defiance, where he settled.

But after a life of travel and adventure Boone could not settle down, and he continued to make hunting and trapping expeditions from his home in Defiance. His last major journey, when he was 80, took him as far as the Yellowstone River in the Rocky Mountains. He died, aged 86, in 1820, honored by the United States Congress as the pioneer who had "opened the way to millions of his fellow men."

The Mississippi river is the background of two of America's most famous children's stories, *The Adventures of Tom Sawyer* and *The Adventures of Huckleberry Finn*. Tom, who is looked after by his strict Aunt Polly, is led into a life of danger and adventure by his friend Huck. The author was Mark Twain, who spent his boyhood in the small town of Hannibal on the Mississippi, about 124 miles (200 kilometers) north of St. Louis. The cliffs, caves, islands and woods along the river at Hannibal form the background to the two stories. Born Samuel Langhorne Clemens in 1835, Mark Twain took his writing name from the call - "Mark twain!" - used by river pilots to check the depth of the water. (It meant that the river was two fathoms, or 12 feet [3.6 meters], deep.) Before he became a writer, Mark Twain spent four years working as a Mississippi river pilot. He wrote about 20 other books before he died in 1910, but *Tom Sawyer* and *Huckleberry Finn* are by far the best known and are still enjoyed today.

OUT OF THE LAKES

THE MIGHTY MISSISSIPPI STARTS LIFE AS A LITTLE STREAM FLOWING OUT OF LAKE ITASCA IN NORTHERN MINNESOTA. AT THIS POINT, IT IS SO SMALL THAT YOU CAN TAKE A FEW STEPS ACROSS IT ON STEPPING-STONES.

▼ *The stepping-stones that mark the spot where the Mississippi leaves Lake Itasca in Minnesota. At this point the river is 1476 feet (450 meters) above sea level.*

LAKE ITASCA IS ONE OF HUNDREDS OF LAKES in northern Minnesota, left behind 10,000 years ago when the glaciers retreated. Streams from these lakes join the Mississippi as it flows slowly on a winding course to Grand Rapids.

This was once a land of tall red and white pine-forests - the home of packs of wolves, herds of elk and colonies of beavers and raccoons. From about 1800 onwards, Native American and European fur-trappers and traders destroyed the wildlife. Then, in about 1830, lumberjacks moved in. Over 16,000 of them, based in camps in the forests, steadily cut down the trees. By 1916, when their log rafts were floated downstream for the last time, there were few trees left. Today, the area has

been replanted and is protected as state and national forest. Wildlife has recovered. Wolves roam the woods again, and beavers build their dams on the forest streams. At Leech Lake, about 25 miles (40 kilometers) from Lake Itasca, 5000 Ojibwe or Chippewa people occupy a reservation to which they were moved in 1867 when their tribal land was cleared for logging.

The upper Mississippi flows through country that experiences a wide range of climates. In January the temperature can fall to -5°F (-20°C). There is frost for up to half the days each year. But in July the temperature can reach 100°F (40°C).

THE TWIN CITIES

Below Grand Rapids, the Mississippi flows on to the northern tip of the Great Plains, which stretch westwards across the United States to the Rockies. This is grain and cattle country. The first big cities on the river are the "Twin Cities" of Minneapolis and St. Paul. The Twin Cities grew up rapidly in the nineteenth century as centers of the timber and flour-milling industries. The last sawmill closed down in 1921 and flour-milling declined in

the 1950s, but St. Paul is still the main river port of the upper Mississippi. Barges (see pages 22-23) set out downriver loaded with grain in the harvest season, scrap iron, salt, coal, chemicals, sand, gravel and other bulk cargoes. The grain that used to be milled into flour at Minneapolis is now carried down the Mississippi to be milled elsewhere. Meanwhile, Minneapolis has become a manufacturing city, the headquarters of international food companies, office equipment manufacturers and electronics companies. With a combined population of 650,000, Minneapolis and St. Paul make up the largest settlement along the Mississippi.

THE LUMBER CAMPS

The lumber, or logging, camps of the nineteenth century were communities where there was little time for anything except work and sleep. Besides lumberjacks who felled the trees and steersmen who guided the log rafts down the rivers, there were craftsmen such as blacksmiths, farriers who looked after the horse-teams and filers who sharpened the saws. The men slept in large bunkhouses, and some had their food brought to them at work on a floating cook shack, or kitchen.

▼ *The beaver was hunted along the streams of the Rockies in the nineteenth century for its fur and meat. An adult beaver grows up to almost 4 feet (1.20 meters) long and weighs up to 55 pounds (25 kilograms).*

THE WORKING RIVER

BELOW MINNEAPOLIS AND ST. PAUL, THE MISSISSIPPI BECOMES A
WORKING RIVER, CHANNELLED, DREDGED AND CONTROLLED SO THAT
IT CAN BE USED BY RIVER BOATS.

BETWEEN THE TWIN CITIES AND ST. LOUIS, near to where the
Mississippi is joined by the Missouri 671 miles (1080
kilometers) downstream, there are 27 locks and dams designed
to allow barges and other river boats to bypass rapids, shallows,
rocks, islands and other hazards. This system of locks and dams
was built in the 1920s and 1930s by United States Army
engineers. The aim was to control flooding and increase the use
of the Mississippi by cargo-carrying barges.

On the Mississippi the channel used by river boats is at least
9 feet (2.75 meters) deep throughout the whole length. It is

WING DAMS

- river bank
- build-up of sediment behind dam
- current
- wing dam

▶ *A bargetow with a cargo of
coal on the Ohio river at
Cincinnati. The Mississippi and
its tributaries make up a vital
transport network, especially for
bulk cargoes.*

◀ *A 25-barge tow on the Mississippi south of St. Louis.*

through the locks in two stages. Below St. Louis, tows sometimes contain up to 50 barges. A tow this size can carry as much cargo as 700 railway cars or nearly 3000 semis. Maneuvering these huge areas of steel from the bridge of a towboat is a highly skilled job, even with modern equipment such as radar and auto-pilots. Sandbanks building up in the channel are a constant threat. In rough weather that whips up the river current, tows often break apart and have to be patiently rounded up and tied together again by the towboat crew. Many tows on the Mississippi carry chemicals, and the risk of pollution or an explosion following a collision is always present.

kept open partly by dredging sediment from the river bed and partly by wing dams or, as they are sometimes called "spur dikes." Wing dams are walls of stone built out from the river banks. They force the water to flow quickly between them, scouring the river bed and washing sediment away from the channel. Where the river meanders as it gets slower and wider, "cut-offs" have been built to take river traffic straight across the bends.

BARGES AND TOWS

River traffic on the Mississippi relies upon its navigable channel being kept free. Bulk cargoes are carried up and downriver by "bargetows." This is a confusing name for them because the barges are not actually towed, but pushed. They are joined together, with thick wire ropes, or hawsers, on each side and in front a diesel-powered towboat or "tug."

North of St. Louis, where bargetows, or tows have to negotiate the locks, they are limited to fifteen barges. Even so, tows with more than nine barges have to be split in two and taken

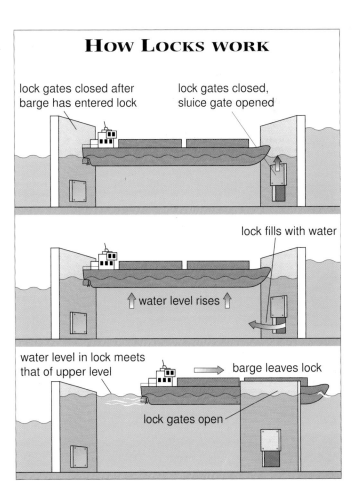

HOW LOCKS WORK

lock gates closed after barge has entered lock

lock gates closed, sluice gate opened

lock fills with water

water level rises

water level in lock meets that of upper level

barge leaves lock

lock gates open

THE MISSOURI

THE WATERS OF THE MISSOURI START THEIR JOURNEY IN THE ROCKY MOUNTAINS — A JOURNEY OF OVER 2486 MILES (4000 KILOMETERS) BEFORE THEY MEET THE MISSISSIPPI NEAR ST. LOUIS.

ON THE EASTERN SLOPES OF THE ROCKIES, 8202 feet (2500 meters) up, is the Yellowstone National Park. This was set up in 1880 as the first of the USA's national parks. Three major rivers flow from it. The Yellowstone heads northeast and joins the Missouri over 621 miles (1000 kilometers) away on the borders of Montana and North Dakota. The two others, the Gallatin and the Madison, flow north through canyons and over waterfalls, which are full in spring when the rain and the meltwater from the mountains combine.

The two rivers meet with a shorter one, the Jefferson, at Three Forks, Montana. Three Forks is the point where the Missouri takes its name, but its source is really in the Yellowstone National Park.

Western Montana is dominated by copper and coal mining. In 1884 the Anaconda Mining Company created the world's

▼*A modern-day cowboy rounds up cattle on the plains of Montana. The days of the great round-ups, when cattle were driven huge distances across country, ended with the arrival of the railways in the mid-nineteenth century.*

◀ *The Castle Geyser in Yellowstone National Park sends hot water fountaining into the sky. Rainwater collects in hot rocks below ground, turns partly to steam and rushes to the surface under pressure.*

largest copper works in the town that gave it its name. The works closed down in 1980, but the scars left behind by copper-mining still spoil the landscape. Elsewhere in Montana large-scale strip, or open-cast, coal-mining has spoilt the landscape too.

THE "BIG MUDDY"

The Missouri flows through northern Montana close to the Canadian border, across the most northerly part of the United States apart from Alaska. On its way across Montana, the Missouri picks up a large number of tributaries. In spring, these rivers carry a huge amount of sediment that is deposited on the river bed and banks as it meets the slower Missouri current. The result is that the Missouri takes a meandering, frequently changing course as its waters try to find a way forward. Riverside trees such as willows and cedars are loosened when the banks are worn away and are carried into the river. Below Fort Peck Lake, a series of dams (see pages 26-27) has now been built to control the flow of sediment in the Missouri, but the river's old nickname, the "Big Muddy," has stuck.

In eastern Montana, the deposits of the Missouri and its tributaries have produced good farming land for both wheat and livestock. Today livestock produces two-thirds of the state's farm income.

ACROSS THE GREAT PLAINS

AFTER CROSSING THE MONTANA STATE BORDER, THE MISSOURI TURNS AND HEADS SOUTH ACROSS NORTH AND SOUTH DAKOTA. FROM HERE TO ST. LOUIS, THE RIVER FLOWS THROUGH THE GREAT PLAINS.

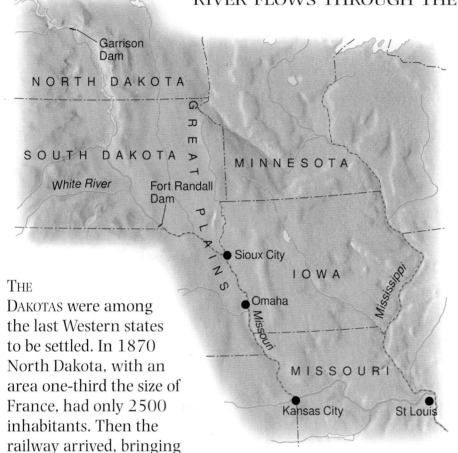

▲ *The "badlands" along the White River, a tributary of the Missouri, in South Dakota. Erosion by wind and water has stripped the land of its soil, so that it can support little plant life. As a result, only a few birds and small animals can survive there.*

THE DAKOTAS were among the last Western states to be settled. In 1870 North Dakota, with an area one-third the size of France, had only 2500 inhabitants. Then the railway arrived, bringing thousands of homesteaders. By 1920 the state population was 646,000, but then the growth stopped. Today, there are 686,000 people living in North Dakota.

THE MISSOURI RIVER BASIN PROJECT

It was a similar story in South Dakota. Homesteaders set up their small farms, fighting against bitterly cold winters and scorching summers to produce wheat, which was the great money-making crop. By the 1930s, the land was exhausted, and some of the top soil had been carried away by the wind. Many farmers went bankrupt. To try to save them, the government began the Missouri River Basin Project. This project involved the building of a series of 7 dams and about 30 smaller ones. They were built along the Missouri, from Fort Peck inside the Montana border to Fort Randall on the border between South Dakota and Nebraska. The entire length of the river valley was flooded. In North Dakota, for example, over 231 square miles (600 square kilometers) of Native American land were taken over and flooded when one of the dams, the Garrison Dam, was built. The Missouri River Basin Project provides hydroelectricity and irrigation for the dry lands on either side, but plans to extend it further have been held up by protests from local people.

◀ *A farmer and child at work on a family farm.*

SOIL EROSION

South of the Fort Randall Dam, the Missouri marks the boundary between Iowa to the east and Nebraska and Kansas to the west. This was an area of great farming prosperity, based on corn and cattle, but erosion of the soil and low world prices for corn and meat have driven many farming families off the land. They have had to try to make a living in the towns instead. With the Missouri as its western border and the Mississippi on the eastern side, Iowa is estimated to have lost half of its top soil - among the best in the world - to the rivers. To keep going, farmers have to use large amounts of chemical fertilizers, which are costly and in the end do permanent damage to the land.

CITIES OF THE MISSOURI

From Sioux City in Iowa, the Missouri is navigable and forms part of the transport

system of the Mississippi basin. The main centers of population between Sioux City and the meeting of the two rivers are places where the railways bridged the river in the nineteenth century, for example Omaha and Kansas City. "Agri-business" - businesses based on farming activities such as grain stores, stockyards and meat-packing plants - grew up at these transport centers. Although other businesses have moved in, the Missouri riverside cities still provide vital services and markets for the farming community.

▶ *Kansas City on the Missouri river is a major center and market for industries based on farming, such as grain-milling and meat-packing.*

THE MEETING OF THE RIVERS

THE MISSISSIPPI AND THE MISSOURI MEET ABOUT 20 MILES (32 KILOMETERS) NORTH OF ST. LOUIS.

THE FORCE OF THE MEETING creates white-topped waves, whirlpools and mushroom-shaped waterspouts that riverboat crews call "boils." The water in midstream is rough enough to break the hawsers holding tows together, so the tows have to creep past close to the shores. Carrying the muddy waters of the Missouri, the Mississippi sweeps round in a 9-mile (15-kilometer) curve called the "Chain of Rocks," where the water is extremely dangerous. A cut-off was built in the 1920s so that river traffic to and from St. Louis could avoid this dangerous area.

THE GATEWAY TO THE WEST

St. Louis was the base from which Lewis, Clark and Pike set out to explore the Missouri and the Upper Mississippi. Later in the nineteenth century, hundreds of thousands of pioneers and homesteaders passed through St. Louis on their way to the West. Farm supplies and farm produce took the same route. Wharves, warehouses, markets and timber-yards stretched for 3.7 miles (six kilometers) along the river bank.

The great days of St. Louis as the "Gateway to the West" are remembered in the stainless steel Gateway Arch, which towers 630 feet (192 meters) above the city beside the river. Completed in 1965, the arch has an elevator to an observation platform where visitors can look over the city.

▼*The Gateway Arch dominates the skyline by the Mississippi at St. Louis. It was designed in the 1960s by the leading American architect Eero Saarinen, whose family moved to the USA from Finland in 1923.*

THE 1993 FLOODS

The 1993 floods were caused by a freak weather pattern over America's Midwest. This brought torrential rain to the region at the same time as the Mississippi's normal floodwater was moving downstream. In June, water began to flow over the flood embankments. By early July towns, cities, and hundreds of farms were under water. Fifty people were killed and 70,000 made homeless. The floods covered almost 17,000 square miles (44,000 square kilometers) of land. The water level began to drop in August, but it was not until September that cleaning-up could start.

Today, with a population of almost 500,000, St. Louis is by far the largest city in the state of Missouri. It is still a key port in the Mississippi and Missouri waterway system, and its good communications have meant other industries, such as petrochemicals and aircraft equipment, have been established there.

THE FLOOD PLAIN

St. Louis marks the divide between the upper and lower Mississippi. To the north, navigation is made possible by the system of locks and dams. The lower river is broad and level enough for riverboats to move more freely, although sandbanks and rocks demand full attention from river pilots.

The river flows past towns like Cape Girardeau and Cairo, towns that saw their great days in the steamboat boom of the nineteenth century but are now quiet and forgotten. Diesel-engined tugs need to make fewer stops for fuel, and small-town wharves are too small for the huge bargetows to use.

From Cairo southwards, the Mississippi is swollen by the waters of the Ohio river. Despite 1988 miles (3200 kilometers) of levees, or flood embankments, which are continually being strengthened and improved, freak weather conditions cause serious floods. In 1927, 1951 and again in 1993 people living along the river had to face the loss of their homes, farms and crops.

COTTON COUNTRY

AS IT FLOWS SOUTH TOWARDS THE
NORTHERN BORDER OF MISSISSIPPI STATE,
THE MISSISSIPPI RIVER ENTERS THE "SUN
BELT," A BROAD BAND ACROSS THE
UNITED STATES, WHICH IS AN
AREA OF GROWING PROSPERITY.

THIS IS COTTON COUNTRY – a group of farming states whose wealth came mainly from growing cotton and also from tobacco and sugarcane. Until slavery was finally abolished in the United States in 1863, most work in the fields was done by slaves from Africa or the West Indies. But cotton no longer needs a large workforce in the fields. Once picked by hand, it has been picked by machines since the 1940s, and one machine operator can do the work of 20 hand-pickers. As a result, many descendants of black slaves found themselves out of work. They either moved away to find new jobs, or went into one of the newer Mississippi industries such as clothing manufacture.

THE COTTON CAPITAL

Memphis, in south-west Tennessee close to the border with Mississippi state, was created by slave labor. In the early nineteenth century, its swamps and woodland were cleared by

▲ *Mud Island, part of the Mississippi River Museum at Memphis, Tennessee, is an exact scale model of the lower Mississippi from Cairo, Illinois to the Gulf of Mexico. It was opened in 1982.*

◀ *A combine-harvester, driven by one operator, harvests a field of cotton. The bolls, or seed-heads, that contain the cotton fiber are stripped from the stems. These are thrown out behind.*

◄ *Beale Street in Memphis, Tennessee, still celebrates its place in the history of American music.*

THE BIRTH OF THE BLUES

Besides being America's "cotton capital," Memphis has played a part in the history of music. The Blues, based on the worksongs sung by black workers in the cotton fields, were first played on Beale Street, Memphis, in 1903 by W. C. Handy. *Saint Louis Blues* is one of his best-known compositions. Fifty years later, a Memphis record producer heard a demo record made by an unknown singer from Tupelo, Mississippi, and liked it. The singer's name was Elvis Presley.

slaves so that a new city could be landscaped. It became, and still is, the center of the American cotton industry, although timber industries such as furniture-making are also important. It also has a vital place in the life of the bargetows. The Waterways Marine is a vast depot which takes fuel, crews, food, newspapers and mail by supply boat to the passing tows. They meet in the middle of the river to avoid the delays of mooring.

▼*Vicksburg's old harbor is now a center for pleasure-boats. Here a fishing boat is moored opposite a modern sternwheeler*

VICKSBURG'S NEW PORT

Unlike Memphis, Vicksburg is a river city that has turned its back on its history of the cotton trade. It was once second only to Memphis in importance, and the older streets are still lined with the mansions of the cotton millionaires of 150 years ago. But Vicksburg's old harbor is now a site for pleasure-boats, and a new commercial port has been built a little way up the Yazoo tributary. The port caters to ocean-going ships as well as Mississippi barges, and it can handle container traffic as well as bulk cargoes such as oil and steel. Although it is about 217 miles (350 kilometers) inland, Vicksburg has turned into a seaport. It has its own Custom House to clear cargoes for import or export.

Vicksburg is also the home of the Waterways Experimental Station, run by the US Army Corps of Engineers. It is responsible for flood control and navigation along the Mississippi. It was set up after the disastrous floods of 1927, which left 750,000 people homeless on the Mississippi flood plain. Its scale models of the entire river, which can reproduce the state of the water at any time of the year, are used to try out new flood-prevention plans before they are built.

THE MISSISSIPPI DELTA

THE MISSISSIPPI REACHES THE GULF OF MEXICO ACROSS A BROAD DELTA OF SWAMPLAND.

THE DELTA IS MADE UP OF SILT brought downstream by the Mississippi and its tributaries. Year after year for many centuries, the river deposited the silt on the river bed and banks. This created the long "neck" of the Mississippi delta, which stretches out into the sea. Behind it, the river made a network of sluggish channels, called "bayous," across the marshes. From time to time, the river overflowed and the floodwater made new creeks and pools.

MANGROVES AND ALLIGATORS

Mangroves, tough evergreen trees whose roots and branches intertwine, form thickets on the marshland, with trails of blue-grey Spanish moss hanging from them. Between the thickets are stretches of reeds and rushes. This habitat is ideal for alligators, flying squirrels, black bears, otters, muskrats and mink, and it provides a summer haven for hundreds of thousands of migrating wild ducks from the north.

CITIES OF THE DELTA

The major city of the delta is New Orleans. About 106 miles (170 kilometers) from the mouth of the Mississippi and so sheltered from

▼ A swamp on the delta. The blue-grey fronds hanging from the trees are Spanish moss. It has no roots in the soil but grows on other plants, and takes its food from the moist air.

◀ *An aerial photograph showing the incoming tide from the Gulf of Mexico. On the right are islands of silt and saltmarsh, formed when marshland is invaded by the sea.*

▶ *A view over the older, central area of New Orleans.*

the sea, it has been an important and prosperous port for over 200 years. In the nineteenth century it became the center of the Mississippi steamship trade, and twelve railways linked the port with the rest of the United States.

The old part of New Orleans was built along a bend in the river. As it grew, it spread on to drained swampland between the river and Lake Pontchartrain. Most of New Orleans is below the Mississippi flood level and is protected by a system of levees and drainage canals.

About 68 miles (110 kilometers) upriver from New Orleans is Baton Rouge, Louisiana's state capital. Until the 1950s it was a small port, but then the river was widened and deepened so that it could be used by oil-tankers. Baton Rouge grew rapidly to become the United States' fourth largest port. Its oil refineries, storage depots and factories make

oil-based products such as chemicals and plastics. The length of the Mississippi between Baton Rouge and New Orleans became known as the "Chemical Corridor" because of pollution leaks into the river and the haze of industrial smoke over the area. Despite stricter controls on industry, these problems continue.

The demand for industrial land has brought prosperity to other cities on the delta. The population of Lafayette has multiplied four times since the 1950s and now numbers 80,000. To the east a new port development, the Port of South Louisiana, has already shot to the top of the league table of US ports, shipping over 50 million more tons of cargo in 1996 than its nearest rival, Houston.

▼*Lush vegetation on the Mississippi delta.*

THE GULF INTRACOASTAL WATERWAY

This canal provides a sheltered route for all types of ships and boats between Cape San Blas in Florida to Galveston, Texas. It crosses the Mississippi delta from near New Orleans to the city of Orange, on the border between Louisiana and Texas. This is a distance of about 404 miles (650 kilometers). The channel is at least thirteen feet (four meters) deep. In the delta it is marked by a line of buoys across the marshland.

PEOPLE OF THE DELTA

HISTORY HAS BROUGHT SETTLERS FROM MANY DIFFERENT COUNTRIES TO THE MISSISSIPPI DELTA. THE RESULT IS A RICH MIXTURE OF CULTURES AND LIFESTYLES.

THE FIRST SETTLERS ON THE DELTA were French. In 1682 France claimed ownership of all the Mississippi valley and called the area Louisiana. It was much larger than the present state of Louisiana and extended as far north as the Canadian border. The French founded New Orleans in 1718 and set up farms and plantations along the bayous. Slaves were brought from Africa and the Caribbean to work in the fields.

In 1762 the king of France gave Louisiana to his cousin, the king of Spain. This began a period of Spanish settlement that continued until 1800, when Louisiana was returned to France. Three years later, France sold the whole area to the United States.

▲ *The Cajun musician Boozoo Chavis plays the accordion at a Cajun Music Festival at Lafayette, Louisiana. Cajun music has fans all over the world.*

MARDI GRAS

The annual festival of Mardi Gras begins in New Orleans on January 6 and continues until Shrove Tuesday, the last day before the Christian season of Lent. The French name *Mardi Gras* means "Fat Tuesday," from the custom of using all the fats before Lent. Parade clubs called krewes organize over 60 parades as well as balls and other events. On the Saturday before Shrove Tuesday, Mardi Gras begins to approach its climax, with marches and processions of decorated floats that continue until Shrove Tuesday itself. Thousands of people take part, but thousands more who come to watch also dress and make up for the occasion.

◀ *Fishing in the delta swamps. Fish is the key ingredient in Cajun cookery.*

These families make a living by farming and cattle-raising, fishing and trapping.

THE MELTING-POT

After Louisiana became American in 1803, many settlers from the eastern states moved south to the Mississippi delta. They were joined later in the nineteenth century by immigrants from Italy, Germany and Ireland. When America freed its slaves in 1863, many African-American families moved off the plantations to find work in New Orleans, which had become one of America's most prosperous cities. New Orleans became a true "melting-pot" of people and customs from all over the Western world. The mixture of cultures in the history of New Orleans makes it one of North America's most exciting and interesting cities. The mixture of Cajun, Creole and Afro-American music with European influences has made New Orleans the world center of jazz, where it began.

CAJUNS AND CREOLES

The early French and Spanish settlers kept themselves apart, keeping their own languages and customs including Roman Catholic church-going. Their descendants, born in Louisiana, became known as Creoles, a word which was also used to describe their black slaves who had been born there.

Another group of French origin, arrived on the delta in 1765. They were French Canadians who had been forced out of Canada by the British. Their Canadian colony had been called *La Cadie*, or the "land of plenty," and they called themselves *Cadiens*. Gradually, the word changed to "Cajuns."

The Cajuns farmed the delta and raised horses and cattle. Many fished in the rich waters of the bayous, and built their homes on stilts above the swamps. Although many Cajuns married people of other ethnic groups, there are still Cajun settlements on the delta.

VISITING THE RIVERS

TOURISTS VISIT THE MISSISSIPPI AND MISSOURI TO EXPLORE HISTORICAL SITES, ENJOY AMERICAN MUSIC, SEE THE WIDE OPEN SPACES OF THE MIDWEST – OR SIMPLY GO FISHING.

◀ *Jazz musicians play on the street at dusk in New Orleans.*

MANY VISITORS EXPLORE THE RIVERS BY BOAT. Hundreds of excursion boats cruise the Mississippi and its tributaries, enabling tourists to recapture the feeling of the days 150 years ago when the only way to reach many remote towns and villages was by river. The most magnificent boats in the cruising fleet are the steam-powered sternwheelers modeled on the boats that carried passengers up and down river in the last half of the nineteenth century. The largest of these, the *American Queen* launched in 1995, can carry up to 420 people on cruises lasting up to two weeks.

◀ *A modern reconstruction of the steam sternwheelers that were a common sight on the Mississippi and its tributaries in the nineteenth century. The* Natchez *takes tourists on extended trips up the Mississippi and Ohio rivers.*

◄ Many of the grand mansions built in the middle of the nineteenth century by farmers and traders who made fortunes out of cotton are major tourist attractions along the Mississippi. This is Rosalie House at Natchez.

states. Both sides fought for command of the Mississippi. Events along the river included a naval battle just north of Memphis in 1862, and the siege of Vicksburg by Northern troops in 1863, which lasted for 47 days until the city surrendered. The siege of Vicksburg is re-enacted every summer.

PALATIAL BUILDINGS

Another magnet for visitors is the splendid nineteenth-century architecture of the riverside towns. Many Mississippi families made fortunes out of the river trade and cotton and built palatial houses for their families. Natchez, in Mississippi state, was a typical prosperous river port. On the cliffs 197 feet (60 meters) above the river, rich landowners and traders built their mansions, often copying Greek or Italian styles of architecture. Many of these are now open to visitors and have been turned into museums. They recreate a way of life that has long since vanished.

THE GREAT RIVER ROAD

Travelers on land can follow the Mississippi down the Great River Road from its source at Lake Itasca all the way to Plaquemine on the delta. This is the most southerly settlement on the river, on the neck of land that juts out into the Gulf of Mexico. The Great River Road is really a collection of state highways and local roads, but special signs with a green and white pilot's wheel symbol highlight the route on both sides of the Mississippi.

Many Americans visit the Mississippi to see historical sites connected with the American Civil War, which was fought from 1861 to 1865 between the Northern and Southern

AMERICAN MUSIC

For many people, the attraction of the Mississippi from St. Louis southwards is tracing the roots of American music. Every September, St. Louis hosts a blues festival. Beale Street in Memphis, the birthplace of the blues, is still famous for its music clubs. In New Orleans, there are dozens of music clubs where traditional New Orleans jazz, Cajun music, blues and country music can be heard. All styles come together each spring in a ten-day "Jazz Fest" to which music-lovers flock from all over the world.

FAIRS AND FESTIVALS

Louisiana's fairs and festivals are main attractions for tourists from other parts of the United States as well as from abroad. Apart from the most famous festival, the Mardi Gras - they include the State Fair at Shreveport in October, the Rice Festival at Crowley in July and the Shrimp Festival at Morgan City in August.

WILDLIFE ON THE RIVER

THE MISSISSIPPI AND MISSOURI FLOW THROUGH A RANGE OF DIFFERENT ENVIRONMENTS FROM THE SUBARCTIC TO THE SUBTROPICAL.

IN THE NORTHERN STATES, there can be as many as five months of deep frost. The temperature of the Mississippi delta, by contrast, rarely falls below 60°F (15°C) and is often above 80°F (30°C).

The wide rivers, with their quiet ox-bow lakes and lagoons, provide a corridor for birds migrating south from Canada for the winter. Snow geese, pelicans, herons, great white egrets, and other waterfowl sweep downriver in thousands as soon as winter approaches. They are joined by large flocks of Monarch butterflies that winter near the Gulf of Mexico.

THE NORTHERN FORESTS

When trappers first explored the northern reaches of the Mississippi and Missouri, they

▲*Waterfowl at Voyageurs National Park in Minnesota. They are on their winter migration route towards the south from the Arctic Circle.*

found a land teeming with wildlife, which could be caught for its fur or its meat. Species included deer, elk, beaver, moose and black bears. The arrival of the trappers meant death for thousands of them. The setting-up of national and state parks in which animal life is protected, and the planting of new trees on cleared land, have resulted in numbers increasing again.The same is true of the plant life of the forests. Tree clearance destroyed the habitats of many mosses, orchids and other species that have now been painstakingly established again in state parks and nature reserves.

◄ The armadillo feeds mainly on insects, although they will also eat roots and worms. If frightened, they burrow quickly into the ground.

CHANGE FOR THE BETTER

Human activity is usually blamed for the destruction of wildlife habitats, but on parts of the Mississippi delta exactly the opposite has happened. Fifty years ago, many creatures such as white-tailed deer and wild turkey, which had once flourished there, were almost extinct. Robbed of their prey, eagles too had disappeared. Then, in the 1950s, marshland trees and shrubs were encouraged to grow between the flood banks to absorb flood water.

These wild areas are now repopulated by deer, grey and red foxes, raccoons, wild turkeys, eagles and the occasional black bear.

There have even been newcomers. The armadillo is a bony-plated mammal native to Mexico and the dry southwestern states of North America. For reasons that still baffle zoologists, thousands of armadillos began a migration to the Mississippi delta about 40 years ago. Although the delta was nothing like their natural habitat, they adapted to it and are now an established delta species.

Another species that has settled on the delta is less welcome. In 1884, some water hyacinths were brought from Brazil to New Orleans, where the beautiful blue-flowered plants were planted in the city's ponds. Within ten years, they had spread into the bayous of the delta, smothering all other plant life with their broad leaves. The fight against the water hyacinth is still going on.

THE MISSISSIPPI ALLIGATOR

The Mississippi alligator is another species of the delta whose numbers are recovering. Up to 13 feet (4 meters) long and weighing up to 992 pounds (450 kilograms), it was hunted almost to extinction for its skin until the 1970s, when it was protected. Today, the alligator population on the delta is estimated at about 500,000.

RIVER OF CHANGE

CORN AND CATTLE IN THE NORTH, AND COTTON IN THE SOUTH, USED TO BE THE MAIN BUSINESS OF THE STATES ALONG THE MISSISSIPPI AND MISSOURI. NOW, NEW INDUSTRIES ARE MOVING IN.

THE MOST IMPORTANT CHANGES came in the south, in the states of Arkansas, Tennessee, Mississippi and Louisiana. The decline of cotton in the south began over 130 years ago, at the end of the American Civil War, and by the 1960s these states were the poorest in the United States. Then their fortunes changed.

▼ *Sorting the shrimp catch at South Pass Port on the Mississippi delta. The level of the sea in the Gulf of Mexico is gradually rising, and saltwater is invading the delta swamps. This has increased the catches of shrimp, crabs and other saltwater species and led to a boom in the Louisiana fishing industry.*

OIL IN THE GULF

The first signs of growth came with the development of the oil and natural gas fields. Between the 1960s and the 1990s, Louisiana has leapt from seventh place to second among the USA's oil-producing states, beaten only by Texas, and from fourth place to first

▲ *Shrimp on their way by conveyor belt to a seafood processing plant at Biloxi, Mississippi, where they will be frozen or canned.*

◄ An oil-drilling platform in the Gulf of Mexico off Louisiana. The Gulf is now one of the busiest offshore oilfields in the world.

world through the thriving Port of South Louisiana. More than 4000 companies are involved in services to the oil industry such as engineering, surveying, supplies and catering.

NEW INDUSTRIES

The oil industry was followed by others. Manufacturers of cars and trucks were looking for "green-field sites" – land away from the cities that had not been built on – for new factories. General Motors built a plant at Spring Hill, south of Nashville, Tennessee, for 7000 workers. This was followed by makers of parts. For example, the Japanese-owned Bridgestone-Firestone tire company moved to Nashville in 1990 from its old base in Akron, Ohio. Close to the Ohio river in Indiana, the Japanese company Toyota opened a new plant in 1995 to make pickup trucks, with smaller factories making engine parts close by.

Meanwhile, Federal Express chose Memphis, on the Mississippi, as its headquarters. This international parcel delivery service employs 20,000 people and is a great boost to the area. Twenty years earlier, no one in the United States would have chosen a city so far south as the hub of a communications network.

Industrial companies are also moving on to sites further north on the Mississippi. One of the largest developments is near Muscatine in Iowa, where the Canadian steel company Ipsco opened a $360 million (£220 million) steel mill in 1996. It could be that in years to come the Mississippi becomes the USA's industrial center.

among producers of natural gas. Until the 1960s, almost all the oil and gas came from wells on land. When these began to run dry, international companies such as Exxon, Standard Oil of California and Gulf started drilling beneath the waters off Louisiana. In their thirst for oil, they went further out into the sea, and today there are thousands of offshore drilling rigs in the Gulf of Mexico. They support the oil and petrochemical industries of the "chemical corridor" between New Orleans and Baton Rouge and supply the

THE FUTURE OF THE MISSISSIPPI

AMONG THE WORLD'S GREAT RIVERS, THE MISSISSIPPI AND MISSOURI
HAVE SEEN THE MOST CHANGE IN THE PAST 100 YEARS.

▲ *Atchafalaya Swamp on the Mississippi delta, which provides a rich habitat for wildlife and good catches for local fishermen. But it could be damaged by flood-prevention plans and encroaching saltwater.*

RIVER ENGINEERS HAVE BUILT dams to make water available for irrigation and hydroelectricity. They have straightened the river's course and built locks to make navigation easier, and they have protected the riverside settlements and farmland with high embankments. One of the results of all this work is that the Mississippi and Missouri, and many of their tributaries, flow faster than before. They carry more sediment downstream, and less is left on the banks and river beds.

THE ENCROACHING SEA

Much of this extra sediment ends up on the Mississippi delta or is carried out into the Gulf of Mexico. There, it is finally deposited when the river current meets the tidal currents of the Gulf. This causes a gradual rise in the level of the sea and the incoming tides bring saltwater further into the freshwater wetlands of the delta.

Only 50 years ago, sediment from the Mississippi was estimated to be adding over one-third of a square mile (one square kilometer) of land to the delta every two years. Now that the sediment is being pushed out further into the Gulf and raising the sea bed, the saltwater is coming back and slowly changing the environment of the swamps. Saltwater species such as shrimp, crabs and lobsters flourish in the salty habitat, but freshwater species such as catfish and perch are forced to retreat upstream. Environmental scientists are worried about the shrinking of the freshwater wetlands, but for delta fishermen the abundance of saltwater fish close inshore is good news. Louisiana supplies a large share of the United States' seafood, and processing it is a major industry.

GLOBAL WARMING

Fears about the long-term future of the lower Mississippi have also been raised by research into global warming. Scientists say that the Earth's atmosphere is getting steadily warmer because of the use of fossil fuels, the destruction of tropical rainforest and chemical pollution. This, they say, will result in the melting of the ice-caps of the Arctic and Antarctic and sea-levels will rise all over the world. Some have forecast a rise of between 7.9 and 15.8 inches (20 and 40 centimeters) over the next 100 years and a possible rise of between 13 and 26 feet (four and eight meters) in later centuries.

An 8 inch (20-centimeter) rise in the Gulf of Mexico would devastate southern Louisiana, including New Orleans. A higher rise would threaten Mississippi state and south-eastern Arkansas. Global warming would also change the climate all over the world. There are already signs that the climate over the Great Plains of the Missouri and upper Mississippi is warmer and drier than it was 100 years ago. However international efforts are being made to reduce the human activities that have led to global warming.

▼*Levees, or flood embankments, along the Mississippi on the edge of New Orleans. The land on each side is below the level of the river and protected only by low embankments.*

GLOSSARY

agri-busness business concerned with crop or livestock farming

archaeologist a person who studies and investigates ancient civilizations

autopilot a device that automatically steers an aircraft or ship

bargetow a group of barges roped together and pushed by a towboat or tug

bayou a slow-flowing stream on a river delta, from the Choctaw Indian word *bayuk*

catfish edible freshwater fish with whiskered mouth

confluence the place where two or more rivers meet

contemporary picture a picture drawn or painted at the time of the event it shows

current the flow of water in a channel

cut-off a short, straight canal cut to bypass bends or shallow places in rivers

delta an area of flat land, made up of silt, where a river meets the sea

descendants later generations of the same family or group of people

erosion the wearing away of rock or soil by the action of wind, ice or water

geyser a hot spring that shoots up into the air from cracks in rocks

glacier a moving sheet of thick ice

hawsers strong, thick ropes that are used as tow-ropes; they are usually made of twisted strands of wire

homesteaders families who traveled west in the United States to set up their own small farms

hot springs streams of hot water flowing from cracks in rocks

hydroelectric power energy produced by converting the energy of falling water into electricity

indigenous people the people who first lived in a country

irrigation distributing water to fields by cutting channels from a river

levees banks alongside rivers, made naturally by sediment or built to prevent flooding

meander winding S-shaped bends of a river

mink a weasel-like animal with long, thick fur that lives near water

muskrat large rodent, similar to a water-rat, which lives near water; also called musquash

navigable wide and deep enough to be used by ships or boats

offshore drilling rig equipment resting on the sea-bed, designed to drill for oil or natural gas under water

ox-bow lake a curved lake formed when a river cuts through the neck of a meander to make a shorter course

petrochemicals substances obtained from oil or natural gas

prairie large area of open grassland without trees

radar an electronic method of detecting distant objects at sea or in the air

round up collecting cattle in large numbers for the journey from the prairies to the market

sediment ground-down pieces of rock and other material carried along by a river and later deposited on the river banks and bed

silt mud and sand deposited at the mouth of a river

sleepers lengths of wood to which railway rails are fixed

strait a narrow sea channel that joins two larger areas of sea

subtropical in an area lying between the hottest, tropical parts of the Earth and the cooler, temperate parts

wetlands areas of swampland that provide habitats for certain species of plant and animal life

INDEX